Contents

AGES 6–7
LITERACY

Premier

QUICK TESTS

Test 1 Letter patterns

Some **letter patterns** are very common.

I can **see** my t**ea**.

I can **row** a bo**a**t.

Choose ee or ea to complete each word.

1. s_____d

2. h_____t

3. k_____p

4. t_____ch

5. f_____st

Choose oa or ow to complete each word.

6. l_____f

7. l_____d

8. c_____ch

9. sh_____

10. narr_____

Colour in your score

Test 2 Word order

We have to write words in the **correct order** so they make **sense**.

eat Monkeys bananas. ☒

Monkeys eat bananas. ☑

Write these sentences correctly.

1. milk. Cats drink _____

2. lay eggs. Birds _____

3. asleep. is dog The _____

4. balloon A pop. can _____

5. is The green. grass _____

6. A hop. frog can _____

7. red. My is coat best _____

8. swim pool. You a in _____

9. wash a You sink. in _____

10. tree tall. very The is _____

Colour in your score

Test 2

Test 3 Adding ing and ed

We can add **ing** and **ed** to the end of some words.

Yesterday I walk**ed** to school.

Today I am walk**ing** to the shops.

Write these words so they end in ing.
Spell them correctly.

1. miss _____

2. shop _____

3. write _____

4. carry _____

5. crash _____

Write these words so they end in ed.
Spell them correctly.

6. beg _____

7. blame _____

8. copy _____

9. splash _____

10. rub _____

School   Shop

10
9
8
7
6
5
4
3
2
1

Colour in your score

Test 3

Test 4 Vowels and consonants

There are **26** letters in the **alphabet**. The five **vowels** are **a**, **e**, **i**, **o** and **u**. All the other letters are called **consonants**.

a	b	c	d	e	f	g	h	i	j	k	l	m
n	o	p	q	r	s	t	u	v	w	x	y	z

Every word usually has **at least one** vowel in it.

Fill in the missing vowel in each word.

1. d____ll

2. sh____ll

3. h____ss

4. sn____p

5. d____ck

6. s____nd

7. k____ng

8. m____sk

9. pr____m

10. sh____e

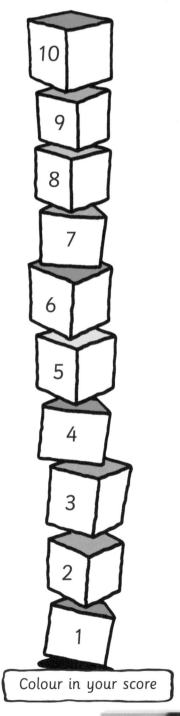

10
9
8
7
6
5
4
3
2
1

Colour in your score

Test 4

Test 5 Making sense of sentences

Sentences must **make sense** when you read them.

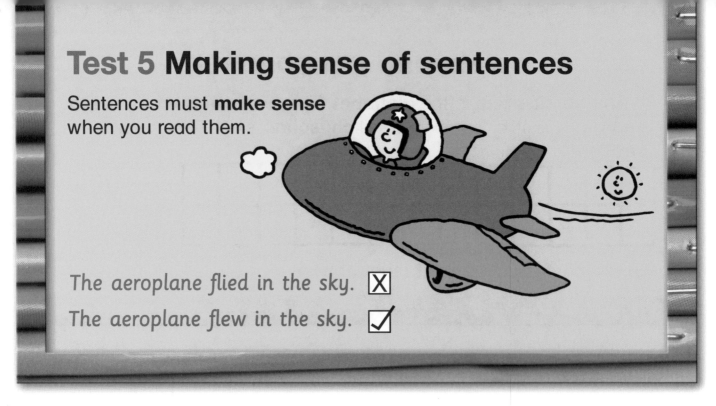

The aeroplane flied in the sky. ☒
The aeroplane flew in the sky. ☑

Choose the correct word to finish each sentence.

1. The dog _____ the postman. (bit/bited)

2. The boy _____ the window. (breaked/broke)

3. I _____ the ball. (catched/caught)

4. I _____ the moon. (seed/saw)

5. The girl _____ reading. (is/are)

6. The children _____ running. (was/were)

7. My mum _____ home. (come/came)

8. I _____ in the shop. (went/goed)

9. I _____ got an apple. (has/have)

10. The boy _____ himself. (hurt/hurted)

Colour in your score

Test 5

Test 6 Conjunctions

A **conjunction** is a **joining** word.
It may be used to join **two**
sentences together.

A mouse is small. An elephant is big.

A mouse is small **but** an elephant is big.

Choose the conjunction and or but to fill each gap.

1. I picked up the apple _____ ate it.

2. The girl found her bag _____ went to school.

3. I got the sum right _____ Ben didn't.

4. The lion stopped _____ roared.

5. I like swimming _____ reading.

6. I sat down _____ watched TV.

7. This door is open _____ that door is shut.

8. Metal is hard _____ wool is soft.

9. I got undressed _____ went to bed.

10. I opened my bag _____ took out a book.

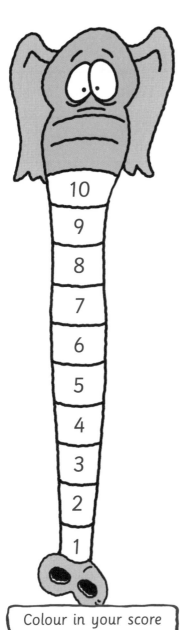

Colour in your score

Test 6

Test 7 Rhyming

Rhyming is important in spelling.

I found a pound on the ground.

I **found** a **pound** on the gr**ound**.

	look	stew	night	
past	head	light	took
	last	new	bread	

Write the five pairs of rhyming words.

1. _____ 2. _____

3. _____ 4. _____

5. _____ 6. _____

7. _____ 8. _____

9. _____ 10. _____

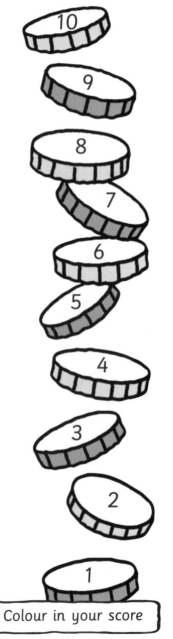

Colour in your score

Test 8 Word building

In spelling we have to learn to **build** up words.

h + ow + l = howl

Do these sums. Write the words you make.

1. l + ou + d = _____

2. d + ow + n = _____

3. m + ou + th = _____

4. f + ou + nd = _____

5. cr + ow + d = _____

6. cl + ow + n = _____

7. sh + ou + t = _____

8. sp + ou + t = _____

9. fl + ow + er = _____

10. cr + ou + ch = _____

Colour in your score

Test 8

Test 9 Full stops and question marks

I live in a house.

Where do you live?

A **sentence** often ends with a **full stop**.

A **question** always ends with a **question mark**.

Rewrite each sentence correctly.

1. a farmer lives on a farm _____

2. why are you late _____

3. bees live in a hive _____

4. what is the matter _____

5. where is my pen _____

6. the fox ran quickly _____

7. the clouds were black _____

8. who is your friend _____

9. the wind is blowing _____

10. how did you do it _____

10
9
8
7
6
5
4
3
2
1

Colour in your score

Test 9

Test 10 Putting words in groups

Sometimes it is helpful to put words into **groups**.

Things that give light

torch   sun   candle   lamp   lantern

Sort these words into groups.

tea	beech	elm	water	oak
ash	coffee	cola	yew	juice

Different sorts of drinks.

1. _____

2. _____

3. _____

4. _____

5. _____

Different sorts of trees.

6. _____

7. _____

8. _____

9. _____

10. _____

Colour in your score

Test 10

Test 11 Antonyms

Antonyms are words that are **opposite** in meaning.

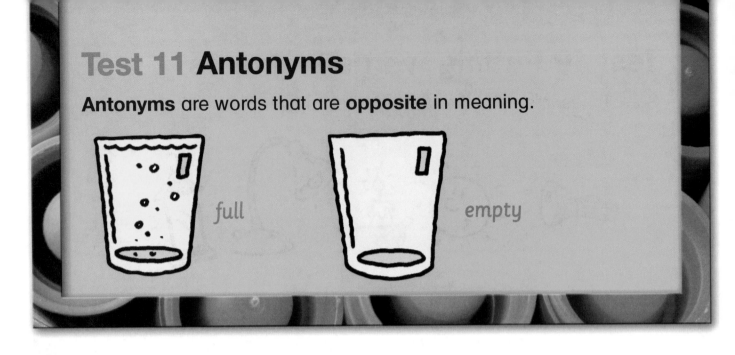

full   empty

Choose the word that means the opposite.

bad	wet	hard	rich	sad
smooth	small	dirty	hot	narrow

1. dry _____

2. poor _____

3. cold _____

4. rough _____

5. easy _____

6. wide _____

7. clean _____

8. good _____

9. big _____

10. happy _____

Colour in your score

Test 11

Test 12 Compound words

Compound words are made up of **two smaller words** joined together.

lady   +   bird   =   ladybird

Do the word sums and write the answers.

1. foot + ball = _____

2. rain + bow = _____

3. sun + shine = _____

4. snow + man = _____

5. play + time = _____

6. butter + fly = _____

7. bull + dog = _____

8. hedge + hog = _____

9. black + berry = _____

10. key + hole = _____

Colour in your score

Test 12

Test 13 Looking carefully at words

We can make new words by **changing some letters**.

cake

rake   **sh**ake   **l**ake

Write the new words you make.

1. Change the **f** in **f**air to **ch**.   _____

2. Change the **r** in **r**are to **fl**.   _____

3. Change the **t** in **t**ear to **b**.   _____

4. Change the **l** in **l**ord to **c**.   _____

5. Change the **j** in **j**aw to **cl**.   _____

6. Change the **c** in **c**ore to **sh**.   _____

7. Change the **w** in **w**ire to **f**.   _____

8. Change the **p** in **p**ure to **c**.   _____

9. Change the **f** in **f**ind to **w**.   _____

10. Change the **r** in **r**oar to **s**.   _____

10

9

8

7

6

5

4

3

2

1

Colour in your score

Test 13

Test 14 Speech marks

Speech marks show someone is speaking. We write everything the person says **inside** the speech marks.

I deliver letters.

The postman said,
"I deliver letters."

Put in the missing speech marks.

1. The builder said, I use a hammer.

2. The driver said, I drive a big lorry.

3. Mrs Smith said, I am feeling tired.

4. The librarian said, I work in a library.

5. The farmer said, I keep cows on my farm.

6. The queen said, I wear a crown.

7. The nurse said, I work in a hospital.

8. The fire-fighter said, My job is dangerous.

9. The caretaker said, I keep the school clean.

10. The baker said, I make bread.

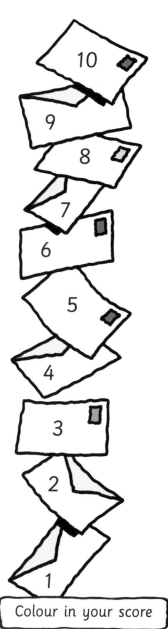

Colour in your score

Test 14

Test 15 **The letters wh and ph**

Two common letter patterns are **wh** and **ph**.

whistle   dolphin

Choose wh or ph to complete each word.

1. ele_____ant

2. _____ere

3. al_____abet

4. _____eat

5. _____ich

6. gra_____

7. ne_____ew

8. _____iskers

9. _____ite

10. _____antom

Colour in your score

Test 15

Test 16 Syllables

When you say a word slowly you can hear that it can be **broken down** into **smaller chunks** called **syllables**.

drag – on

(two syllables)

Tap out the syllables when you say each word.

Say these words slowly.
Does each word have two or three syllables?

1. elephant _____

2. phantom _____

3. slowly _____

4. syllable _____

5. alphabet _____

6. hairdresser _____

7. drummer _____

8. watering _____

9. inside _____

10. replied _____

Colour in your score

Test 16

Test 17 Verbs

Verbs tell us what someone is **doing**.

*A cow **moos**.*

Choose the best verb to complete each sentence.

moos	clucks	purrs	neighs	hoots
grunts	gobbles	bleats	quacks	barks

1. A cow _____.

2. An owl _____.

3. A hen _____.

4. A duck _____.

5. A turkey _____.

6. A horse _____.

7. A dog _____.

8. A sheep _____.

9. A pig _____.

10. A cat _____.

Colour in your score

Test 18 Beginnings and endings

Always make sure your **sentences make sense**.

Sam has forgotten to finish her sentence.

Ben has rubbed out the beginning of his sentence.

My pencil...

... watched television.

Join up the beginning and ending of each sentence.

1. The farmer

in the stable.

2. The horse was

are cold.

3. Some birds

drives a tractor.

4. My pencil

is shut.

5. Ice-creams

were singing in the tree.

6. In my garden

is curly.

7. The door

is sharp.

8. I am eating

I grow flowers.

9. My hair

is on.

10. The television

some chips.

Colour in your score

Test 19 **The letters er, ir and ur**

The letter patterns **er**, **ir** and **ur** make a similar sound.

fern   shirt   purse

Choose er, ir or ur to complete each word.

1. d_____ty

2. k_____b

3. t_____n

4. sh_____t

5. s_____ve

6. n_____se

7. c_____ve

8. st_____

9. b_____d

10. t_____m

Colour in your score

Test 19

Test 20 Checking your sentences

Always check your writing to see if you have
made any silly mistakes.

goes
The rocket ~~go~~ fast.

Choose the correct word to complete each sentence.

1. My uncle _____ very nice. (is/are)

2. The birds _____ very noisy. (was/were)

3. The children _____ reading. (is/are)

4. The girl _____ asleep. (was/were)

5. The cat _____ milk. (like/likes)

6. I _____ it well. (did/does)

7. My cousin _____ to visit. (comed/came)

8. I _____ my shirt. (teared/tore)

9. Tom always _____ hard at maths. (try/tries)

10. Lions _____. (roar/roars)

10
9
8
7
6
5
4
3
2
1

Colour in your score

Test 20

Test 21 Looking for letter patterns

The letter pattern **ea** has two sounds.

I can r**ea**d a book.

ea sounds like **ee**
(as in r**ee**d)

Yesterday I r**ea**d a comic.

ea sounds like **e**
(as in r**e**d)

Divide these words into sets.

seat	cheat	ready	sweat	feather
head	bread	teach	meal	clean

Write the words in which **ea** sounds like **ee** as in r**ee**d.	Write the words in which **ea** sounds like **e** as in r**e**d.
1. _____	6. _____
2. _____	7. _____
3. _____	8. _____
4. _____	9. _____
5. _____	10. _____

Colour in your score

Test 21

Test 22 Commas

Commas are used to **separate** things in a **list**.
We **don't** use a comma before the word **and**.

sheep, duck, pig and hen

Fill in the missing commas.

1. red yellow blue and green

2. lion tiger cheetah and leopard

3. apples pears bananas and grapes

4. pen pencil crayon and felt-tip

5. rain sun snow and fog

6. I saw a car a bus a lorry and a bike.

7. In my bag I took a mirror a ruler and a pencil.

8. I like oranges peaches cherries and melons.

9. I can play football cricket rugby and snooker.

10. A gardener needs a spade a fork a trowel and a hoe.

Colour in your score

Test 23 Adding to the ends of words

Sometimes we can change words by **adding letters** to the **end** of them.

The kitten likes to **play**. It is very play**ful**.

When **full** comes at the end of a word we spell it **ful**.

Do these word sums. Write the answers.

1. use + ful = _____

2. hope + ful = _____

3. help + ful = _____

4. pain + ful = _____

5. thank + ful = _____

Take off ful. Write the word you are left with.

6. colourful _____

7. faithful _____

8. truthful _____

9. cheerful _____

10. careful _____

Colour in your score

Test 23

Test 24 Questions

A **question** should begin with a **capital letter** and end with a **question mark**.

What is this?

Write each question correctly.

1. who looks after our teeth
   _____

2. what flies in the sky
   _____

3. where is your shirt
   _____

4. what do we use to dig with
   _____

5. who lives next door to you
   _____

6. where do we get milk from
   _____

7. why are you crying
   _____

8. how did you do that
   _____

9. who is your best friend
   _____

10. what makes a seed grow
    _____

Colour in your score

Test 24

Test 25 Exclamation marks

We use an **exclamation mark** when we feel **strongly** about something.

What a mess!

Rewrite each sentence. End each sentence with either a question mark or an exclamation mark.

1. come quickly _____

2. who are you _____

3. when did you arrive _____

4. stop messing about _____

5. what a nice surprise _____

6. what are you doing _____

7. you are horrible _____

8. this cake tastes good _____

9. why are you so upset _____

10. shut that door _____

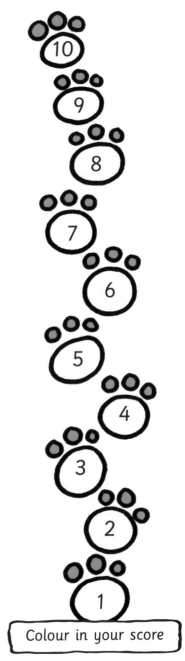

Colour in your score

Test 25

Test 26 Singular and plural

Singular means **one** thing. **Plural** means **more** than one thing.

one sweet   lots of sweets

Complete each of these.

1. one rabbit, lots of _____

2. one chocolate, lots of _____

3. one tree, lots of _____

4. one cap, lots of _____

5. one chair, lots of _____

6. one _____ , lots of plates

7. one _____ , lots of horses

8. one _____ , lots of cakes

9. one _____ , lots of rockets

10. one _____ , lots of dragons

Colour in your score

Test 27 Capital letters

We use a capital letter to **begin** the names of **people**, the names of **days of the week** and **months of the year**.

My name is Shanaz.

My birthday is in March.

Write and spell correctly, the name of some months.

The name of the months begining with J.

1. _____   2. _____

3. _____

The name of the months ending with ber.

4. _____   5. _____

6. _____   7. _____

The name of the months begining with A.

8. _____   9. _____

The name of the month begining with F.

10. _____

Colour in your score

Test 27

Test 28 Synonyms

Synonyms are words with **similar meanings**.

I'm **quick**.

I'm **fast**.

Write the word that has a similar meaning.

damp	upset	closed	dislike	talk
bored	large	go	high	difficult

1. big _____

2. hate _____

3. speak _____

4. leave _____

5. angry _____

6. tall _____

7. fed up _____

8. shut _____

9. wet _____

10. hard _____

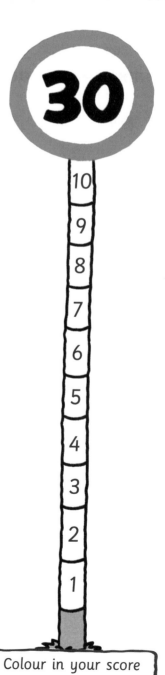

30

10
9
8
7
6
5
4
3
2
1

Colour in your score

Test 28

Test 29 Collecting words

We can **group** some words together because they are all **related**.

shirt   jeans   jumper   coat

These are all names of **clothes**.

Underline the odd word out in each group.

1. cricket football book swimming

2. pen arm leg head

3. potato carrot onion sun

4. bridge table chair wardrobe

5. rabbit drums trumpet guitar

6. car bus lorry library

7. daisy bluebell grasshopper buttercup

8. oak bite ash lime

9. telephone London Cardiff Glasgow

10. sheep lion cow hen

Colour in your score

Test 29

Test 30 Checking up on punctuation

Punctuation marks make writing **easier** to read.

It's raining.

Sam said It's raining ☒

Sam said, "It's raining." ☑

Fill in all the missing punctuation marks in these sentences.

1. The boy got up

2. Where is my dinner

3. Get out of my way

4. I love maths science reading and sports.

5. May I come with you

6. My dog is black

7. Anna said, I'm hungry

8. What a horrible day

9. My bike has a flat tyre, Tom said.

10. How many questions are there

Colour in your score

Test 30

ANSWERS

Test 1
The missing letters are in **bold**.
1. s**ee**d
2. h**ea**t
3. k**ee**p
4. t**ea**ch
5. f**ea**st
6. l**oa**f
7. l**oa**d
8. c**oa**ch
9. sh**ow**
10. narr**ow**

Test 2
1. Cats drink milk.
2. Birds lay eggs.
3. The dog is asleep.
4. A balloon can pop.
5. The grass is green.
6. A frog can hop.
7. My best coat is red.
8. You swim in a pool.
9. You wash in a sink.
10. The tree is very tall.

Test 3
1. missing
2. shopping
3. writing
4. carrying
5. crashing
6. begged
7. blamed
8. copied
9. splashed
10. rubbed

Test 4
The missing vowel is in **bold**.
1. d**o**ll
2. sh**e**ll
3. h**i**ss
4. sn**a**p
5. d**u**ck
6. s**a**nd
7. k**i**ng
8. m**a**sk
9. pr**a**m
10. sh**oe**

Test 5
1. bit
2. broke
3. caught
4. saw
5. is
6. were
7. came
8. went
9. have
10. hurt

Test 6
1. and
2. and
3. but
4. and
5. and
6. and
7. but
8. but
9. and
10. and

Test 7
1. look
2. took
3. stew
4. new
5. night
6. light
7. past
8. last
9. head
10. bread

Test 8
1. loud
2. down
3. mouth
4. found
5. crowd
6. clown
7. shout
8. spout
9. flower
10. crouch

Test 9
1. A farmer lives on a farm.
2. Why are you late?
3. Bees live in a hive.
4. What is the matter?
5. Where is my pen?
6. The fox ran quickly.
7. The clouds were black.
8. Who is your friend?
9. The wind is blowing.
10. How did you do it?

Test 10
1. tea
2. water
3. coffee
4. cola
5. juice
6. beech
7. elm
8. oak
9. ash
10. yew

Test 11
1. wet
2. rich
3. hot
4. smooth
5. hard
6. narrow
7. dirty
8. bad
9. small
10. sad

Test 12
1. football
2. rainbow
3. sunshine
4. snowman
5. playtime
6. butterfly
7. bulldog
8. hedgehog
9. blackberry
10. keyhole

Test 13
1. chair
2. flare
3. bear
4. cord
5. claw
6. shore
7. fire
8. cure
9. wind
10. soar

Test 14
1. The builder said, "I use a hammer."
2. The driver said, "I drive a big lorry."
3. Mrs Smith said, "I am feeling tired."
4. The librarian said, "I work in a library."
5. The farmer said, "I keep cows on my farm."
6. The queen said, "I wear a crown."
7. The nurse said, "I work in a hospital."
8. The fire-fighter said, "My job is dangerous."
9. The caretaker said, "I keep the school clean."
10. The baker said, "I make bread."

Test 15
The missing letters are in **bold**.
1. ele**ph**ant
2. **wh**ere
3. al**ph**abet
4. **wh**eat
5. **wh**ich
6. gra**ph**
7. ne**ph**ew
8. **wh**iskers
9. **wh**ite
10. **ph**antom

Test 16
1. three
2. two
3. two
4. three
5. three
6. three
7. two
8. three
9. two
10. two